A Home at Mount Vernon

by Jonathan Stein

 HOUGHTON MIFFLIN HARCOURT
School Publishers

PHOTOGRAPHY CREDITS: **Cover** (t) Stockbyte/Getty Images. (b) © George and Monserrate Schwartz/Alamy. **Title Page** The Granger Collection, New York. **3** The Granger Collection, New York. **5** © Bettmann/CORBIS. **7** Private Collection/Peter Newark American Pictures/The Bridgeman Art Library. **10** The Granger Collection, New York. **11** Cameron Davidson/ Workbook Stock/Jupiterimages. **13** The Granger Collection, New York. **14** © George and Monserrate Schwartz/Alamy. **15** © Richard T. Nowitz/CORBIS.

Printed in China

ISBN-13: 978-0-547-01660-3
ISBN-10: 0-547-01660-3

6 7 8 9 0940 18 17 16 15 14 13
4500396626

A Trip to the Capital

It's a hot, humid summer day in Washington, D.C. Suppose that you and your family are visiting the nation's capital, and you've been here for several days. The sticky weather is uncomfortable. You've toured the Capitol, the building where Congress makes laws. Perhaps you watched the House of Representatives debate a bill about establishing a new national park. Or maybe you toured the White House, visiting rooms where history was made. You've seen the gleaming white tower of the Washington Monument; the Lincoln Memorial, where a marble statue of Lincoln watches over the city; and the long black wall of the Vietnam Veterans Memorial.

On the next-to-last day of your visit, your family drives across the Potomac River and heads south into Virginia toward a place called Mount Vernon. This was George Washington's true home. As you wind your way through Virginia, your dad announces he's going to read part of a biography of George Washington.

"Hey," you say, "I already know about George Washington, the father of our country. First in war. First in peace. First in the hearts of his countrymen."

"Good," your dad says. "But I bet there are some things you don't know." Opening a thick book, he begins to read from a chapter titled "Surveying the Land."

Young George Washington surveyed land on the frontier.

This is what your dad reads:

In 1743, when George Washington was 11, his father died. Instead of going to Europe to complete his education as the sons of other Virginia planters did, George remained at home to help his mother on the plantation.

When Washington was about 15, he began working as a surveyor, a person who measures areas of land to establish boundaries. His understanding and love of the land grew. He noticed that parts of the Potomac River were too wild to navigate. The young Washington saw the advantages of building canals that went around the roughest portions of the river, allowing both transportation and the development of farmland. It became a lifelong goal to build canals along the Potomac.

"I never knew Washington built canals," you say.

"Neither did I," says your dad. "This next chapter is about when he was a teenager." Here is what your dad reads next:

During his teenage years, Washington spent a great deal of time with his older half-brother Lawrence, who owned Mount Vernon. When Lawrence died in 1752, Washington went to live at Mount Vernon. He also took Lawrence's place in the Virginia militia. A year later, the Virginia governor sent Major Washington as an ambassador to meet with French and Indian traders along the Ohio River. Washington's mission was to tell the traders to leave because Virginia had a claim to the land.

The next year, Washington led Virginia troops on a mission to enforce the colony's claim to the land on the Ohio River. He suffered a humiliating defeat when he had to surrender to a larger French force. This was the beginning of the French and Indian War. Later in the war, Washington volunteered as an aide to General Edward Braddock, who had been sent by Great Britain to remove the French from the Ohio Valley. The young officer showed great courage and skill during battle. For his bravery, Washington was rewarded with the command of all of Virginia's forces. He was learning how to be a leader in a time of war.

"So Washington fought in another big war before the American Revolution?" you remark.

"Yes, and not only that," says your dad. "He was fighting alongside the British, not against them. Listen to this…"

"During the French and Indian War, Washington fought alongside British-born officers. These men considered themselves superior to the "colonials." As a result, they treated Washington with contempt. Washington may have begun to feel the stirrings of resentment toward the British.

In 1758, Washington resigned his commission as an officer and returned to Mount Vernon. He spent the next 15 years living the life of a farmer and plantation owner. He married Martha Custis and served in the House of Burgesses, Virginia's legislative body.

Even though he spent these years in peace, Washington was aware of the rumblings against the British. In 1765, Great Britain passed the Stamp Act, which put a tax on virtually every piece of printed paper. Washington told a friend that Parliament "has no more right to put their hands into my pocket, without my consent, than I have to put my hands into yours for money."

Patrick Henry, a Virginia Patriot, spoke out against British rule in the House of Burgesses.

Washington's resentment toward Great Britain grew. He felt that the British Parliament considered American interests less important than those of the "mother country."

In 1774, Washington was convinced that Virginia's liberties were being threatened by the actions of the British Parliament. Great Britain had passed several laws that came to be known as the "Intolerable Acts." According to one of these acts, British officials could now treat American colonists however they liked without fear of being tried for crimes in a colonial court. One of the Intolerable Acts, the Québec Act, actually took land away from the colonies by extending the Canadian border southward. Virginians' outrage at this law angered the British governor of the colony, Lord Dunmore. He closed the House of Burgesses.

Matters quickly came to a head. Rebellious Virginia lawmakers, including George Washington, held a meeting at the Raleigh Tavern in Williamsburg. They wanted to prohibit British goods from entering the colonies. They proposed a boycott against the importation of goods such as tea and sugar. They also called for a meeting to be attended by representatives from each of the colonies. Washington was one of seven delegates from Virginia chosen to attend the new congress.

The First Continental Congress met in Philadelphia in the fall of 1774. Delegates from all the colonies except Georgia attended. There were some fiery speeches calling for independence. But in the end, the delegates agreed to ask the British Parliament to repeal the Intolerable Acts and, based on Britain's response, to meet again the *following year. George Washington returned to Virginia and began to organize companies of militia in the northern part of the colony to be ready in case they were needed.*

Washington attended the Second Continental Congress, which took place in June of 1775, also in Philadelphia. By this time, the first shots of the Revolutionary War had been fired at Lexington and Concord, in Massachusetts. The delegates to the congress chose Washington to be commander in chief of the Continental Army. He humbly accepted the position, declaring that he would not take any payment for his service. He immediately set out for Boston to assume his command.

Washington accepted command of the American forces.

★　　★　　★

Mount Vernon is only about a 30-minute drive from Washington, D.C. While your dad is reading about Washington taking command of American forces, the car is getting closer to Mt. Vernon. Before you know it, you're almost there.

Now the car turns onto a road that leads through forested countryside toward the large estate overlooking the Potomac River. The scenery is marvelous—beautiful trees and rolling hills.

"This was George Washington's world," your dad says dramatically. "Here, you'll meet the real person—the quiet, private man who felt most at home on his estate, the man who thought of himself first and foremost as a farmer. If we find a turnout on this road, we can read more about Washington and the Revolutionary War."

Your mom finds a place to pull over and stop the car. Now it is her turn to read.

This is what your mother reads:

At first, Washington's troops had success against the British. They celebrated a victory at Fort Ticonderoga in 1775. This success was of great benefit in recruiting more troops and bringing in supplies and money for the American forces.

In 1776, Washington's Continental Army captured Boston. Soon after, however, the Americans lost New York and were nearly defeated. Washington knew that he had very little time left to produce a victory. His soldiers' tours of duty were almost up, and without a victory to build morale, many of them would just go home. On a freezing Christmas night in 1776, Washington's army crossed the Delaware River into New Jersey. They surprised the British and, against all odds, won an important victory at Trenton. Washington followed that up with a victory at Princeton, New Jersey. These two victories were crucial. They boosted morale within the army and also helped the public feel more confident about the war's outcome. Washington was starting to understand that public support was important to the war effort.

The British also learned something. They were beginning to see that a determined and dedicated Washington was not going to surrender. The British would have to completely destroy the Continental Army to end the American Revolution.

Cornwallis surrendered to Washington at Yorktown.

Washington's army spent the freezing winter of 1777–1778 at Valley Forge, Pennsylvania. Many soldiers starved or died of exposure. In the midst of brutal conditions, Washington stayed with his men. He was often seen riding through the camps, encouraging his troops.

During the next few years of the war, American troops experienced both victories and setbacks. In 1781, France sent an army and part of its navy to help the American cause. With their help, Washington was able to trap British General Charles Cornwallis at Yorktown, Virginia. The British surrender at Yorktown effectively marked the end of the Revolutionary War.

Throughout the war, Washington's military leadership was remarkable. He held together the entire Continental Army. Washington worked with the Continental Congress and each individual colonial government to recruit and supply his troops. He even found ways to win support from other countries. Despite *the fact that his army often seemed on the verge of coming apart at the seams, he kept it together through his calm determination.*

In 1783, on the anniversary of the Battle of Lexington, Washington's officers gathered at Fraunces Tavern in New York City. The great leader was on his way to offer his resignation from the army in order to return to his home at Mount Vernon. Washington wanted to meet with his officers one last time and say farewell before he retired from public life. Unashamed to show their tears, they begged him to continue as their leader. Washington, though touched by their love and loyalty, refused. He intended to enjoy the peace of Mount Vernon and to resume his life as a gentleman farmer.

Mount Vernon sits on a bluff overlooking the Potomac River.

For the next four years, Washington stayed out of politics. Yet he continued to keep himself informed about how the new nation was faring under the Articles of Confederation, the first document that spelled out how the state and national governments would share power.

In 1787, Washington returned to public service. He objected to weaknesses in the Articles that gave more power to the individual states than to the nation as a whole. He presided over the Constitutional Convention, where the Constitution was drafted, debated, and finally accepted by the 13 states. The Constitution provided the structure of government and basic rule of law that governs America to this day.

Finally, your family arrives at the parking lot at Mount Vernon. Mount Vernon, you discover, is beautiful and peaceful. The mansion sits on a bluff, surrounded by gardens and fields. Some farming is still done at Mount Vernon, using the same methods that Washington employed.

Before entering Mount Vernon, your family eats lunch at a restaurant with furnishings similar to those that were the style in Washington's time. Even the waiters are in colonial dress. While you are eating lunch, your mother reads the last section from the book about George Washington. Here is what she reads:

After the Constitutional Convention, Washington returned to Mount Vernon once again, but his stay was only temporary. In 1789, the man who wanted simply to return to a peaceful private life became the nation's first President.

One of Washington's most important goals was to make sure that the new nation would not become involved in any foreign wars, a policy that stood firm for over 100 years. He also set up a national bank. When some contrary Pennsylvanians rose in rebellion against federal taxes, he led the forces that put the rebellion down. In 1795, he worked successfully to establish a peace treaty with Great Britain.

George Washington posed for this portrait as the first President of the United States.

Washington served as president for two four-year terms, refusing a third. In his Farewell Address, he called on his fellow citizens to love the nation, avoid becoming divided over issues, and avoid permanent alliances with other countries.

Mount Vernon

After leaving office, Washington returned to Mount Vernon for good. At last, the opportunity came to devote his life to what he loved the most. He was extremely interested in new farming methods and experimented constantly with better ways to raise his crops. He thought of himself as a "scientist of farming." Washington documented his results by recording the work done in his fields, and eventually became one of the most prominent farmers in the new United States.

George and Martha Washington lived at Mount Vernon for the rest of their lives. Washington died there on December 14, 1799, after catching a chill while riding around his farms. He and Martha are buried on the estate.

The restored kitchen of Mount Vernon

After lunch, you take a guided tour of the mansion. You are struck by the low ceilings, and think that perhaps people were shorter back then. Then you remember that Washington was more than six feet tall, and you wonder if he had to stoop. Many of the furnishings are from Washington's time.

One of the things you learn gives you an idea of how Washington dealt with a personal problem. You had heard that Washington had wooden teeth. In fact, he did have problems with his teeth. When Washington was President, his false teeth were made out of hippopotamus and elephant ivory. They were held together with springs. Teeth from humans and donkeys were also inserted in some of his dentures! Maybe that's why Washington was never pictured with his mouth open. Imagining how uncomfortable the dentures must have been, you are thankful for modern dentistry.

During your tour, you learn that Mount Vernon had been in Washington's family for more than 100 years before he inherited it. In 1674, George's great-grandfather bought and began to develop the property. George's grandfather sold about half the estate, but held onto the land at Little Hunting Creek. George's father, Augustine, moved his family onto the estate in 1735. George's half-brother, Lawrence, took over the land in the 1740s. After Lawrence died, the estate eventually passed to George. Lawrence named the plantation "Mount Vernon" in honor of a famous British war hero, Vice Admiral Edward Vernon. Lawrence had served under Vernon in a war between

Britain and Spain. George never changed the name, even though it honored an Englishman.

When George Washington inherited the mansion, it was a simple farmhouse consisting of two floors. There were four rooms on the first floor and three bedrooms on the second. Soon he began to expand the house, eventually doubling its size. He raised it from one-and-a-half stories to two-and-a-half before his marriage. Just before the Revolutionary War, he added north and south wings. After the war, he added a large dining room.

After the tour, you and your family roam about the estate. Forty-five acres of the plantation are open to the public. There are beautiful gardens. Some of the trees were actually planted in Washington's time. You visit a four-acre "demonstration farm," exploring the 16-sided "treading barn" where grain was threshed, and wander around the fields.

People who work on the farm wear 18th-century costumes. They run the farm today as if it were still a profitable business. People cook in the old manner, in wood-burning stoves. In the gristmill, grains such as wheat and rye are ground into flour. A 16-foot waterwheel powers the grinding operations. You decide that modern technology has a lot to recommend it.

The plantation seems vast. Perhaps you walk along the forest trail and relax in the shade of the trees. You cross a wooden footbridge spanning a steep ravine. Signs along the way describe animals that once lived there.

One thing that saddens you is discovering that more than 300 enslaved African Americans worked at Mount Vernon during Washington's time. The sobering fact that slavery existed on almost all Virginia plantations does not seem like an excuse. However, you learn that Washington left instructions in his will that all the people enslaved at Mount Vernon were to be freed after his wife's death. You wonder what became of them.

Later, you and your family take a boat tour on the Potomac River, where you can see the mansion from below the bluff. Afterwards, you return to the grounds of Mount Vernon.

Your time at Mount Vernon has come to an end. The sun is beginning to set, and your family piles into the car for the trip back to the nation's capital. It has been a long day, and you have learned a lot. Previously, George Washington was a figure from the distant past. He seems now a living man—one whom it would have been an honor to know.

Responding

✓ **TARGET SKILL** **Fact and Opinion** Think about the facts and opinions the author includes about George Washington's home at Mount Vernon. Then copy the chart below. Add facts and more opinions to the chart.

Fact	Opinion
?	The gardens are beautiful.

Write About It

Text To World In 1783, Washington resigned from the army. Four years later, he returned to public life. Write a few paragraphs summarizing why Washington first resigned and then returned to public duty.

advantages	previously
benefit	prohibit
contrary	rebellious
midst	repeal
objected	temporary

EXPAND YOUR VOCABULARY

delegates	resignation
militia	surveyor

✔ **TARGET SKILL** **Fact and Opinion** Decide whether an idea can be proved or is a feeling or belief.

✔ **TARGET STRATEGY** **Question** Ask questions about a selection before you read, as you read, and after you read.

GENRE **Narrative Nonfiction** gives factual information by telling a true story.